My Book

This book belongs to

*Name:*_____

Cover Design by :
Gowri Vemuri

First Edition :
January, 2019

Author :
Gowri Vemuri

Edited by :
Raksha Pothapragada

Questions: mathknots.help@gmail.com

This book is dedicated to:

My Mom, who is my best critic, guide and supporter.

To what I am today, and what I am going to become tomorrow,

is all because of your blessings, unconditional affection and support.

This book is dedicated to the

strongest women of my life ,

my dearest mom

and

to all those moms in this universe.

G.V.

School and College Ability Test (SCAT)

John Hopkins University, Center for Talent Search **(CTY)** offers enriched/advance programs during academic year and summer for children from grade 2-12. To get enrolled into these programs, **CTY conducts a screening test (SCAT), which is designed above grade level to challenge the kids.** Student scores are compared to the other students at the same and above grade level.

Based on child's test scores, CTY recommends advanced courses that they offer during academic year and summer. High scoring students are also recognized at a CTY awards ceremony.

SCAT Test Format

The SCAT test comprises of Verbal and Quantitative sections, each section has 55 questions.

Verbal Section measures a student's understanding of the meaning of words and relationship between them. Multiple-choice Questions are given. Students are required to identify the analogy between pair of words and complete the analogy from the given choices.

Quantitative Section measures mathematical reasoning ability of students. Students are required to compare the quantities and determine, whether two values are equal, or one is greater or lesser over the other. They all need to identify if the information provided is sufficient to solve the problem.

SCAT test categories :

Grades	Test Level (Grades)	Verbal Scoring Range	Quantitative Scoring Range	Test Timing/Breaks
2-3	4-5	401-471	412-475	Each section 22 mins with 10 min break
4-5	6-8	405-482	419-506	Each section 22 mins with 10 min break
6 and above	9-12	410-494	424-514	Each section 22 mins with 10 min break

       www.math-knots.com

Scoring Process:

Score will be based on the number of questions the student answers correctly out of the 50 scored questions in each section. Scores are compared against higher grade score. For example, Grade 2 students are compared to a general population of 4th graders, Grade 3 to Grade 5, Grade 4 to Grade 6, Grade 5 to Grade 8, Grade 6 to Grade 9, Grade 7 to Grade 12 and Grade 8 to Grade 12.

Student Grade	Test Level (Grades)	Scores compared Grade	Minimum scores for Qualification (Verbal)	Minimum scores for Qualification (Quantitative)
2	4-5	4	>=430	>=435
3	4-5	5	>=435	>=440
4	6-8	6	>=440	>=450
5	6-8	8	>=445	>=465
6	9-12	9	>=450	>=470
7	9-12	12	>=455	>=475
8	9-12	12	>=460	>=480

INTERPRETING YOUR CHILD'S TEST RESULTS:

Level and Form: There are different difficulty levels and forms of the SCAT. Difficulty levels are tied to a student's grade in school. Research has shown that grades are more closely related to academic performance than students' age. The "Level and Form" code is a record of exactly which test your child took on the indicated test date.

Raw Score: The raw score is the number of questions your child answered correctly out of 50. On each of the two subtests, there are 50 items that count toward the total raw score.

Scaled Score: CTY uses the scaled score to compare the performance of students taking various forms of the test and to determine eligibility for programs and awards. Scaled scores range from 400 to 514 depending on the subtest and level of the test.

Percentile: The percentile shows how your child's results compare to a sample of students from the general population that are in a higher, comparison grade. For example, a 7th grade test-taker in the 63rd percentile compared to grade 12 means the 7th grader scored

better than or equal to 63 percent of a sample of 12th graders. More specifically, it is estimated

that this student may be able to reason better than or equal to 63 percent of 12th graders but

not that they know more than or equal to 63 percent of 12th graders.

TEST TAKING TIPS:

These are general tips for taking the SCAT :

- Make sure you eat and drink well before the test. Hungry and thirsty brains can't think well.

- Have few scratch papers and pencils ready though it is a computer-based test it will be helpful.

- Remember you are taking above grade level test.

- Time is the essence of finishing the test.

- If you are spending much time on a question move on.

- If you can't answer a question, move on and not worry much. If possible, make a note on the scratch paper so that you can revisit the question at the end. You can come back later to answer time permitting by pressing the PREVIOUS button.

- For the questions you want to recheck If possible, make a note on the scratch paper so that you can revisit the question at the end. You can come back later to answer time permitting by pressing the PREVIOUS button.

- Read the question and all multiple choices before answering.

- There is no penalty for wrong answers, so guessing is OK.

- Remember: Rechecking is resolving the problem again.

- Finally, be confident, and good luck!

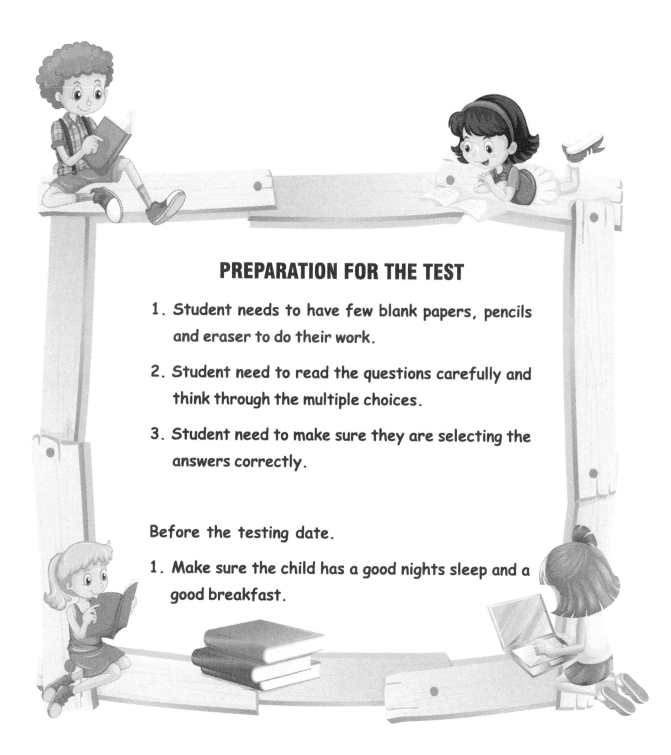

PREPARATION FOR THE TEST

1. Student needs to have few blank papers, pencils and eraser to do their work.

2. Student need to read the questions carefully and think through the multiple choices.

3. Student need to make sure they are selecting the answers correctly.

Before the testing date.

1. Make sure the child has a good nights sleep and a good breakfast.

www.math-knots.com

PART - I
VERBAL ANOLOGIES

INSTRUCTIONS:

All the questions in verbal analogies are to be answered following the below question (instruction).

The first two words are related in a certain way as the next two words. <u>Identify the missing word or analogy.</u>

www.math-knots.com

www.math-knots.com

Sample   The first two words are related in a certain way as the next two words. Identify the missing word.

Clouds : White :: Sky : ?

A. Bold   B. Blue   C. Silver   D. Yellow

Solution : B

First analogy is color of the clouds which is white. Color of sky is blue.

Right choice is B.

Student needs to think through how the first two are related and then relate it to next analogy in the same way. Bubble the correct option.

www.math-knots.com

1. **Ship**   :   **Water**   ::   **?**
    A. Airplane   :   Sky
    B. Concrete   :   Road
    C. Travel   :   Luggage
    D. Gate   :   Wood

2. **Deer**   :   **Grass lands**   ::   **?**
    A. Den   :   Fish
    B. Kennel   :   Cat
    C. Stable   :   Dolphin
    D. Bull   :   Cattle Shed

3. **Hand**   :   **Fingers**   ::   **?**
    A. Ankle   :   Nail
    B. Knee   :   Ear
    C. Feet   :   Toes
    D. Arm   :   Leg

4. **Ocean**   :   **Surfing**   ::   **?**
    A. Soccer Ball   :   Baskets
    B. Basket Ball   :   Kicks
    C. Bricks   :   Hot
    D. Sand   :   Castles

5. **Trees**   :   **Green**   ::   **?**
    A. Sky   :   Blue
    B. Plane   :   Wide
    C. Clouds   :   Gloomy
    D. Rain   :   Cyclone

                                       www.math-knots.com

6. **Shorts**   :   **Summer**   ::   ?
    A. Miami   :   Alaska
    B. Leaves Falling   :   Spring
    C. Fur Coat   :   Winter
    D. Shorts   :   Snow man

7. **Summer**   :   **June**   ::   ?
    A. Spring   :   April
    B. Winter   :   June
    C. Spring   :   September
    D. Summer   :   December

8. **Mosquito**   :   **Blood**   ::   ?
    A. Bees   :   Wax
    B. Virus   :   Metal
    C. Leaves grow   :   Winter
    D. Termites   :   Wood

9. **Numbers**   :   **Math**   ::   ?
    A. Grammar   :   Vowels
    B. Punctuation   :   Consonants
    C. Alphabets   :   Reading
    D. Game   :   Briley

10. **Camera**   :   **Pictures**   ::   ?
    A. Pixel   :   Pixar
    B. Paintbrush   :   Painting
    C. Draw   :   Numbers
    D. Frame   :   Construct

11. **Spring**   :   **Leaves Grow**   ::   **?**
     A. Leaves   :   Fruits
     B. Flowers Bloom   :   Winter
     C. Harvesting   :   Flowers
     D. Fall   :   Leaves Fall

12. **Sun**   :   **Day**   ::   **?**
     A. Moon   :   Night
     B. Afternoon
     C. Dusk
     D. Morning

13. **Owl**   :   **Owlet**   ::   **?**
     A. Calf   :   ankle
     B. Moan   :   Cat
     C. Deer   :   Fawn
     D. Cub   :   Camel

14. **Solo**   :   **One**   ::   **?**
     A. Quadra   :   Five
     B. Duet   :   Two
     C. 4   :   Triplet
     D. Twice   :   One

15. **Echinoderms**   :   **5 legs**   ::   **?**
     A. Penta   :   Six legs
     B. Tri   :   Four legs
     C. Uno   :   Two legs
     D. Deco pods   :   Ten legs

16. **Bank**   :   **Money**   ::   ?
   A. Computers   :   Papers
   B. Library   :   Books
   C. Food   :   Service
   D.

17. **Bury**   :   **Cover**   ::   ?
   A. Open   :   Hide
   B. Open   :   Turn
   C. Dig   :   Uncover
   D. Twist   :   Close

18. **Decade**   :   **10 Years**   ::   ?
   A. Century   :   One Hundred Years
   B. One Million Years   :   Platinum Jubilee
   C. Five Hundred Years   :   Century
   D. Thousand years   :   Silver Jubilee

19. **Father**   :   **Dad**   ::   ?
   A. Grand Ma   :   Mother
   B. Grand   :   Grand Mother
   D. Dads Dad   :   Brother
   C. Grand father   :   Grand Pa

20. **Circle**   :   **Zero**   ::   ?
   A. Septagon   :   Seven
   B. Quadra   :   Three
   C. Pentagon   :   Four
   D. Nanagon   :   Five

 www.math-knots.com

21. **Bark** : **Brown** :: ?
    A. Yellow : Hard
    B. Orange : Sky
    C. Leaves : Green
    D. Pale : Bright

22. **Goose** : **Water** :: ?
    A. Rabbit
    B. Burrow
    C. Sty
    D. Trees

23. **Bus** : **Road** :: ?
    A. Ship : Road
    B. Sub Marine : Water
    C. Flight : Sail
    D. Train : Sky

24. **Basket Ball** : **Baskets** :: ?
    A. Soccer ball : Goals
    B. Tennis : Fouls
    C. Basket Ball : Runs
    D. Swimming : Hits

25. **Green** : **Go** :: ?
    A. Stop : Orange
    B. Blue : Slow
    C. Red : Stop
    D. Detour : Black

www.math-knots.com

26. **Winter** : **December** :: **?**
    A. Columbus Day : May
    B. Fall : October
    C. April : Veteran's Day
    D. August : 31 days

27. **Pear** : **Trees** :: **?**
    A. Pumpkin : Vine
    B. Shrubs : Trees
    C. Under Ground : Straw Berries
    D. Plants : Pears

28. **Hen** : **Chick** :: **?**
    A. Cub : Lamb
    B. Kid : Girl
    C. Giraffe : Calf
    D. Pup : Kitten

29. **Rabbit** : **Kit** :: **?**
    A. Colt : Bolt
    B. Fish : Fry
    C. Infant : Baby
    D. Cub : Cat

30. **Reptiles** : **4 legs** :: **?**
    A. Fish : 8 legs
    B. Animals : 2 legs
    C. 6 legs : Insects
    D. Amphibian : 4 legs

31. **Manometer**   :   **Air pressure**   ::   ?
     A. Magnetisam   :   Voltage
     B. Magento graph   :   Magnetic Field
     C. Length   :   Wide
     D. Current   :   Attract

32. **Legs**   :   **Walk**   ::   ?
     A. Wings   :   Fly
     B. Still   :   Move
     C. Roll   :   Flap
     D. Hands   :   Run

33. **Note**   :   **Music**   ::   ?
     A. Alphabets   :   A
     B. Print   :   Number
     C. Read   :   Write
     D. Letters   :   Words

34. **Mammals**   :   **Four Legs**   ::   ?
     A. Cow   :   Eight Legs
     B. Insects   :   Four legs
     C. Insects   :   Six Legs
     D. Pig   :   Two legs

35. **Map**   :   **Fold**   ::   ?
     A. Globe   :   Spin
     B. Coin   :   Bounce
     C. Paper   :   Toss
     D. Bird   :   Hold

23

36. **Trash**   :   **Garbage**   ::   **?**
    A. Trash   :   Clean
    B. Pollute   :   Nice
    C. Energy   :   Food
    D. Recycle   :   Reuse

37. **Couple**   :   **Two**   ::   **?**
    A. Double   :   Two
    B. Uno   :   Triple
    C. Trio   :   Quadruple
    D. Octa   :   5

38. **Mom**   :   **Mother**   ::   **?**
    A. Pa   :   Ma
    B. Maa   :   Dad
    C. Grand Pa   :   Grand Ma
    D. Granny   :   Grand Mother

39. **North**   :   **South**   ::   **?**
    A. South   :   North West
    B. East   :   West
    C. East   :   West North
    D. East South   :   East West

40. **Car**   :   **Four Wheels**   ::   **?**
    A. Two Wheels   :   Truck
    B. Bicycle   :   Three Wheels
    C. Car   :   Eight Wheels
    D. Tri Cycle   :   Six Wheels

41. **Base Ball** : **Runs** :: ?
    - A. Score : Count
    - B. Bat : Hits
    - C. Tennis : Points
    - D. Soccer : Runs

42. **Zoo** : **Elephant** :: ?
    - A .Cat : Den
    - B. Bees : Trees
    - C. Dog : Jungle
    - D. Nest : Bird

43. **Monkey** : **Trees** :: ?
    - A. Coop : Cat
    - B. Hen : Kennel
    - C. Bee Hive : Birds
    - D. Web : Internet

44. **White** : **Peace** :: ?
    - A. Angry : Blue
    - B. Smile : Grumpy
    - C. Black : Sad
    - D. Anxious : Crying

45. **Feather** : **Light** :: ?
    - A. Feather : Bird
    - B .Flare : Twist
    - C. Glint : Light
    - D. Mountain : Heavy

46. **Labor Day**   :   **September**   ::   **?**
     A. Christmas   :   December
     B. October   :   M.L.K Day
     C. May   :   Columbus Day
     D. July   :   Thanks Giving

47. **Triangle**   :   **Three**   ::   **?**
     A. Pentagon   :   Four
     B. Hexagon   :   Six
     C. Polygon   :   Eight
     D. Five   :   5

48. **Apple**   :   **Trees**   ::   **?**
     A. Bushes   :   Apples
     B. Plants   :   Pumpkins
     C. Under Ground   :   Plums
     D. Grapes   :   Vines

49. **Basket Ball**   :   **Throw**   ::   **?**
     A. Push   :   Pull
     B. Soccer Ball   :   Kick
     C. Basket Ball   :   Hit
     D. Tennis Ball   :   Catch

50. **Lemon**   :   **Sour**   ::   **?**
     A. Fruits   :   Spicy
     B. Candy   :   Tangy
     C. Chocolate   :   Sweet
     D. Ice Cream   :   Bland

26

51. **Duck** : **Duckling** :: ?
    A. Giraffe : Cub
    B. Hen : Chick
    C. Cat : Calf
    D. Donkey : Herd

52. **Head** : **Hat** :: ?
    A. Ears : Ear Plugs
    B. Coat : Legs
    C. Hat : Feet
    D. Cotton : Dress

53. **Helmets** : **Bicycles** :: ?
    A. Train : Road
    B. Tricycle : Belt
    C. Bike : Swim
    D. Seat Belts : Car

54. **Thermometer** : **Temperature** :: ?
    A. Current : Past
    B. Anemometer : Wind Speed
    C. Distance : Ruler
    D. Torque : Fly

55. **Sunglasses** : **Summer** : ?
    A. Gloves : Winter
    B. Fall : Coat
    C. Autumn : Leaves Grow
    D. Spring : Leaves Fall

56. **Donkey**   :   **Stable**   ::   ?
    A. Kennel   :   Cat
    B. Burrow   :   Dog
    C. Goat   :   Pen
    D. Coop   :   Rat

57. **10**   :   **Number**   ::   ?
    A. Words   :   Consonant
    B. Numbers   :   Writing
    C. Language   :   Speak
    D. A   :   Alphabet

58. **Pentagon**   :   **5**   ::   ?
    A. Polygon   :   7
    B. Quadrilateral   :   4
    C. Triangles   :   5
    D. Double   :   3

59. **Gold**   :   **Yellow**   ::   ?
    A. Tree   :   Green
    B. Orange   :   Leaves
    C. Bark   :   Red
    D. White   :   Carpet

60. **Thermometer**   :   **Temperature**   ::   ?
    A. Humidity   :   Rain
    B. Wind   :   Fly
    C. Rain Gauge   :   Precipitation
    D. Sky   :   White

61. **Wings** : **Birds** :: ?
   - A. Birds : Blue
   - B. Sparrow : Nest
   - C. Ladybug : Kennel
   - D. Fins : Fish

62. **Thanks giving** : **November** :: ?
   - A. Memorial Day : May
   - B. December : Summer
   - C. April : Columbus Day
   - D. February : Christmas

63. **Up** : **Down** :: ?
   - A. Corner : Turn
   - B. Below : Under
   - C. Above : Sky
   - D. Right : Left

64. **Cow** : **Calf** :: ?
   - A. Spider ling : Insect
   - B. Cat : Kitten
   - C. Foal : Fuel
   - D. Ducklet : Swim

65. **Insects** : **6 legs** :: ?
   - A. Octopus : 8 legs
   - B. Insect : 5 legs
   - C. 10 legs : Cows
   - D. 12 legs : Fishes

66. **Medicines** : **Pharmacy** :: ?
   A. Book Store : Printer
   B. School : Books
   C. Food : Restaurant
   D. Office : Café

67. **Ship** : **Water** :: ?
   A. Road : Boat
   B. Sky : Sub Marine
   C. Sub Way : Truck
   D. Train : Track

68. **Telescope** : **Magnification** :: ?
   A. Accelerometer : Acceleration
   B. Magnetometer : Voltage
   C. Survey : Surf
   D. Electricity : Magnetic Field

69. **Christmas** : **Christmas Tree** :: ?
   A. Turkey : Christmas
   B. Green : Halloween
   C. Labor Day : Black
   D. July Fourth : Fire Crackers

70. **Green** : **Spinach** :: ?
   A. Tomato : Green
   B. Orange : Carrot
   C. Peppers : White
   D. Banana : Brown

www.math-knots.com

71. **Zebra** : **Stripes** :: ?
    A. Lady Bug : Dots
    B. Solid color : White
    C. Zig Zag : Dots
    D. Lines : Parallel

72. **Hurricanes** : **Ocean** :: ?
    A. Storm : Earth quake
    B. Waves : Rain
    C. Tornado : Land
    D. Sky : Swim

73. **Lion** : **Roar** :: ?
    A. Elephant : Trumpet
    B. Horse : Grunt
    C. Bird : Squeak
    D. Hen : Bleat

74. **Blustery** : **Windy** :: ?
    A. Pleasant : wind
    B. Cold : Frigid
    C. Dawn : Night
    D. Volcano : Water

75. **Digestion** : **Stomach** :: ?
    A. Stomach : Fat
    B. Legs : Crawl
    C. Eyes : Close
    D. Hear : Circulation

76. **Repair**   :   **Broken**   ::   **?**
      A. Selfish   :   Kind
      B. Foreign   :   Alien
      C. Mean   :   Express
      D. Nasty   :   Disgusting

77. **Verdict**   :   **Judgement**   ::   **?**
      A. Novice   :   Skilled
      B. Evil   :   Good
      C. Graceful   :   Elegant
      D. Vicious   :   Humane

78. **Accident**   :   **Collision**   ::   **?**
      A. Clean   :   Septic
      B. Popular   :   Favorite
      C. Immortal   :   Infinite
      D. Spooky   :   Unexcitable

79. **Eat**   :   **Apple**   ::   **Drink**   :   **?**
      A. Think
      B. Supper
      C. Breakfast
      D. Milk

80. **Game**   :   **Play**   ::   **Bike**   :   **?**
      A. Vacation
      B. Ride
      C. Energy
      D. Person

81. **Ocean**   :   **Wave**   ::   **Tree**   :   **?**
    A. Branch
    B. Lawn
    C. Office
    D. Bush

82. **Clue**   :   **Mystery**   ::   **Door**   :   **?**
    A. Close
    B. Open
    C. Key.
    D. Home

83. **Egg**   :   **Chicken**   ::   **Milk**   :   **?**
    A. Cow
    B. Butter
    C. Barn
    D. Yogurt

84. **Swim**   :   **River**   ::   **Climb**   :   **?**
    A. Playing
    B. Music
    C. Ready
    D. Tree

85. **Grimace**   :   **Pain**   ::   **Smile**   :   **?**
    A. Suffer
    B. Sad
    C. Pleasure
    D. Hurt

                     www.math-knots.com

86. **Tornado** : **Wind** :: **Rain** : **?**
   A. Ocean.
   B. Water
   C. Summer
   D. March

87. **Doctor** : **Operation** :: **Lawyer** : **?**
   A. Books
   B. Trial
   C. Jail
   D. Punishment

88. **Chocolate** : **Dessert** :: **Pumpkin** : **?**
   A. Pimples
   B. Taste
   C. Sour
   D. Pie

89. **Vine** : **Grapes** :: **Tree** : **?**
   A. Farmer
   B. Roses
   C. Apple
   D. Farms

90. **Rod** : **Fishing** :: **Gun** : **?**
   A. Crime.
   B. Safety
   C. Cops.
   D. Shoot

www.math-knots.com

91. **Remote** : **Close** :: **Alien** : **?**
    A. Stranger
    B. Remote
    C. Native
    D. Safe

92. **Food** : **Dish** :: **Fruits** : **?**
    A. Leaves
    B. Basket
    C. Trash
    D. Empty

93. **Spring** : **Rain** :: **Winter** : **?**
    A. Snow
    B. Wet
    C. Flurries
    D. Fall

94. **Clock** : **Time** :: **Ruler** : **?**
    A. Watch
    B. Inches
    C. Weight
    D. Length

95. **Quarrel** : **Rival** :: **Fight** : **?**
    A. Knowledge
    B. Thief
    C. Enemy
    D. Enjoy

www.math-knots.com

96. **Brim** : **Hat** :: **Shoelace:** ?
    A. Shoe
    B. Sandals
    C. Shade
    D. Knots

97. **Doctor** : **Hospital** :: **Waiter** : ?
    A. Office
    B. Leafy
    C. Town
    D. Restaurant

98. **Sorrow** : **Cry** :: **Happy** : ?
    A. Weeping
    B. Smile
    C. Teeth
    D. Grumpy

99. **Right** : **Left** :: **Up** : ?
    A. Far
    B. Straight
    C. Side
    D. Down

100. **Play** : **Stage** :: **Movie** : ?
    A. Screen
    B. Script
    C. Audience
    D. Props

www.math-knots.com

101. Helmets   :   **Bicycles**   ::   **Seat belts**   :   **?**
- A. Accidents
- B. Head
- C. Cars
- D. Outside

102. Greenhouse Gases : **Earth**   ::   **Heater**   :   **?**
- A. Warm
- B. Home
- C. Temperature
- D. Climate

103. Horse   :   **Foal**   ::   **Cat**   :   **?**
- A. Tricks
- B. Pony
- C. Puppy
- D. Kitten

104. Snow   :   **Snowboarding** ::   **Concrete**   :   **?**
- A. Skateboarding
- B. Mountain
- C. Competition
- D. Skis

105 Call   :   **Cell phone**   ::   **Email**   :   **?**
- A. Internet
- B. Computer
- C. Key board
- D. Wi Fi

          www.math-knots.com

106. **Tricycle**   :   **Triangle**   ::   **Octagon** :   **?**
   A. Octopus
   B. Shape
   C. Polygon
   D. Sides

107. **Tomatoes**   :   **Plant**   ::   **Potatoes** :   **?**
   A. Underground
   B. Vegetable
   C. Vines
   D. Healthy Fries

108. **Diseases**   :   **Bacteria**   ::   **Rotten**   :   **?**
   A. Raw
   B. Clean
   C. Utensils
   D. Fungus

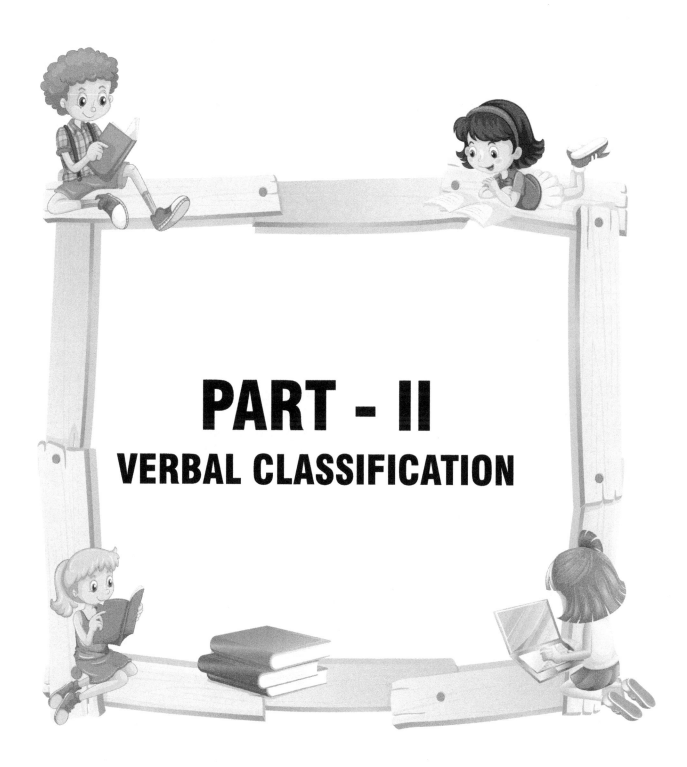

PART - II
VERBAL CLASSIFICATION

www.math-knots.com

INSTRUCTIONS:

All the questions in verbal classification are to be answered following the below question (instruction).

Three words are related in a certain way. Four options are given. Identify the choice that <u>does not belong</u> to the group ?

www.math-knots.com

Sample

Three words are related in a certain way. Four options are given. Identify the choice that does not belong to the group ?

One   Two   Three

A. Six
B. Eight
C. Five
C. Gate

Solution : D

Three words in the question belong to one group. One of the four choices doesn't belong to the same group. Identify and bubble the correct choice. In the given question all three in first row are words as well as numbers in words. Lets take a look at the answers. All choices are words but three are numbers in words and one other word gate, which is incorrect.

www.math-knots.com

109. Dress   **Shorts**   **Tie**

    A. Umbrella

    B. Pant

    C. Socks

    D. Shirt

110. Earthquakes   **Hurricane**   **Catastrophe**

    A. War

    B. Tornado

    C. Blizzard

    D. Floods

111. Yellow   Orange   Green

    A. Red

    B. Blue

    C. Color

    D. Orange

112. Eyes   **Nose**   **Hearing**

    A. Skin

    B. Tongue

    C. Sound

    D. Teeth

113. Nitrogen   **Helium**   **Oxygen**

    A. Carbon dioxide

    B. Zone

    C. Hydrogen

    D. Ozone

www.math-knots.com

114. Awesome   Fantastic   Happy
  A. Lively
  B. Ecstatic
  C. Joy
  D. Gloomy

115. Gold   Bronze   Iron
  A. Mercury
  B. Copper
  C. Steel
  D. Tin

116. Shoulder   Hip   Fingers
  A. Knee
  B. Palm
  C. Ankle
  D. Elbow

117. Lawyer   Professor   Doctor
  A. Engineer
  B. Fire Fighter
  C. Journalist
  D. Learner

118. Mentor   Coach   Principal
  A. Professor
  B. Teacher
  C. Student
  D. Tutor

119. **Viola**   **Guitar**   **Sitar**
  A. Violin
  B. Tabla
  C. Cello
  D. Harp

120. **Creek**   **River**   **Brook**
  A. Runnel
  B. Pond
  C. Stream
  D. Spring

121. **Twig**   **Branch**   **Flower**
  A. Trunk
  B. Tree
  C. Fruit
  D. Root

122. **Train**   **Helicopter**   **Bus**
  A. Transport
  B. Airplane
  C. Cab
  D. Ferry

123. **Skiers**   **Wrestler**   **Jockey**
  A. Archers
  B. Boxers
  C. Player
  D. Rowers

124.   **Freedom**   **Admission**   **Sanction**
   A. Permit
   B. Agree
   C. Consent
   D. Confess

125. **Fence**   **Door**   **Desk**
   A. Fire Wood
   B. Wood
   C. Tooth Picks
   D. Deck

126. **Climax**   **Vertex**   **Zenith**
   A. Pack
   B. Acme
   C. Crest
   D. Peak

127. **Cave**   **Stable**   **Kennel**
   A. Burrow
   B. Den
   C. Canoe
   D. Hive

128. **Neptune**   **Pluto**   **Venus**

   A. Mars
   B. Uranus
   C. Earth
   D. Moon

www.math-knots.com

129. **Rhombus**   **Triangle**   **Square**
   A. Cone
   B. Circle
   C. Rectangle
   D. Trapezoid

130. **Airplane**   **Glider**   **Helicopter**
   A. Kite
   B. Radar
   C. Bird
   D. Rocket

131. **Calf**   **Kitten**   **Chick**
   A. Fawn
   B. Pup
   C. Cub
   D. Pig

132. **Mother**   **Daughter**   **Aunt**
   A. Son
   B. Grand Mother
   C. Niece
   D. Sister In Law

133. **Tree**   **Bush**   **Shrub**
   A. Vine
   B. Plant
   C. Leaf
   D. Creeper

134. **Monopoly**   **Ping-Pong**   **Cards**
    A. Chess
    B. Polo
    C. Squash
    D. Bowling

135. **Tax**   **Dues**   **Levy**
    A. Invoice
    B. Quotation
    C. Bill
    D. Liability

136. **Yam**   **Onion**   **Turnip**
    A. Potato
    B. Carrot
    C. Ginger
    D. Spinach

137. **Attorney**   **Lawyer**   **Judge**
    A. Liquidator
    B. Advocate
    C. Barrister
    D. Counselor

138. **Cutter**   **Sword**   **Rapier**
    A. Knife
    B. Dagger
    C. Arrow
    D. Spear

139. **July**   January   August
   A. March
   B. April
   C. December
   D. October

140. **Ice-Cream**   Yogurt   Custard
   A. Milk
   B. Cheese
   C. Butter
   D. Whip Cream

141. **Support**   Footing   Base
   A. Foundation
   B. Bottom
   C. Underlying
   D. Exterior

142. **Eye**   Thumb   Kidney
   A. Lung
   B. Knee
   C. Nose
   D. Shoulder

143. **Basket Ball**   Hockey   Soccer
   A. Soccer
   B. Billiard
   C. Tennis
   D. Lacrosse

144. **Namib**   **Black Rock**   **Sahara**
     A. Europe
     B. Atacama
     C. Thar
     D. Antarctic

145. **Australia**   **Africa**   **Asia**
     A. North America
     B. London
     C. Europe
     D. Antarctica

146. **Cottage**   **Bungalow**   **Farm House**
     A. Palace
     B. Manor
     C. Villa
     D. Portico

147. **Ear**   **Hand**   **Leg**
     A. Heart
     B. Lower Limb
     C. Nail
     D. Cheek

148. **Arithmetic**   **Fractions**   **Decimals**
     A. Geometry
     B. Algebra
     C. Mathematics
     D. Calculus

149. **Dollar**   **Pound**   **Dinar**
    A. Peso
    B. Rupee
    C. Money
    D. Euro

150. **Adorned**   **Ornate**   **Elaborate**
    A. Showy
    B. Fancy
    C. Beautify
    D. Dull

151. **Honey**   **Amber**   **Gold**
    A. Mustard
    B. Teal
    C. Banana
    D. Lemon

152. **Boar**   **Bull**   **Dog**
    A. Duck
    B. Buck
    C. Rooster
    D. Tiger

153. **Prism**   **Cube**   **Cylinder**
    A. Cone
    B. Sphere
    C. Pyramid
    D. Pentagon

154. **Look**   **Scan**   **Glimpse**
    A. View
    B. See
    C. Wink
    D. Gaze

155. **Friendship**   **Affection**   **Harmony**
    A. Closeness
    B. Intimacy
    C. Fondness
    D. Animosity

156. **Ring**   **Watch**   **Bangle**
    A. Armlet
    B. Tiara
    C. Wristband
    D. Charm

157. **Actress**   **Hero**   **Actor**
    A. Performer
    B. Artist
    C. Heroine
    D. Producer

158. **Earth**   **Venus**   **Moon**
    A. Milky way
    B. Sun
    C. Neptune
    D. Jupitar

159. **Apple**   **Mango**   **Cherry**
   A. Orange
   B. Potato
   C. Plum
   D. Grapes

160. **Cricket**   **Flea**   **Beetle**
   A. Scorpion
   B. Bug
   C. Hopper
   D. Insect

161. **Perfect**   **Present**   **Future**
   A. Past Future
   B. Progressive
   C. Interrogative
   D. Future Simple

162. **Chlorine**   **Neon**   **Sulphur**
   A. Nitrogen
   B. Iodine
   C. Radon
   D. Lead

163. **Axe**   **Sickle**   **Spade**
   A. Farming
   B. Rake
   C. Shovel
   D. Hoe

164. Lime   **Mint**   **Neon**

    A. Emerald

    B. Olive

    C. Jade

    D. Crimson

165. Strength   **Vigor**   **Courage**

    A. Muscle

    B. Might

    C. Cowardice

    D. Firm

166. Book Case   **Book Rack**   **Dresser**

    A. Coat Rack

    B. Quilt

    C. Chest

    D. Ottoman

167. Mother   **Father**   **Daughter**

    A. Son

    B. Brother

    C. Sister

    D. Friend

168. Turtle   **Snake**   **Chameleon**

    A. Rabbit

    B. Crocodile

    C. Dinosaur

    D. Lizard

169. Screw Driver   **Axe**   **Hammer**
- A. Lean
- B. Scissors
- C. Shovel
- D. Chisel

170. Physics   **Social**   **Math**
- A. English
- B. Biology
- C. Subjects
- D. Chemistry

171. Lead   **Chalk**   **Ink**
- A. Pencil
- B. Crayon
- C. Pen
- D. Marble

172. Saw   **Clamps**   **Spade**
- A. Dibber
- B. Nail
- C. Axe
- D. Plough

173. Gallon   **Pint**   **Cup**
- A. Gram
- B. Tablespoon
- C. Ounce
- D. Quart

174. **Dictionary**   **Novel**   **Magazine**
   A. Newspaper
   B. Stories
   C. Comics
   D. Thesis

175. **Ant**   **Caterpillar**   **Moth**
   A. Insect
   B. Spider
   C. Scorpio
   D. Wasp

176. **Crow**   **Pigeon**   **Sparrow**
   A. Cuckoo
   B. Parrot
   C. Duck
   D. Robin

177. **Mile**   **Foot**   **Yard**
   A. Meter
   B. Inch
   C. Quart
   D. Centimeter

178. **Mature**   **Grown**   **Ripen**
   A. Complete
   B. Young
   C. Final
   D. Ready

179. **Pistachio**   **Almond**   **Cashew**
   A. Pecan
   B. Macadamia
   C. Walnuts
   D. Beans

180. **Branch**   **Thorn**   **Leaves**
   A. Tumor
   B. Bud
   C. Needles
   D. Graft

                   www.math-knots.com

VERBAL APTITUDE
ANSWER KEYS

www.math-knots.com

1.   A

2.   D

3.   C

4.   D

5.   A

6.   C

7.   A

8.   D

9.   C

10.   B

11.   D

12.   A

13.   C

14.   B

15.   D

16.   B

17.   C

18.   A

19.   D

20.   A

21.   C

www.math-knots.com

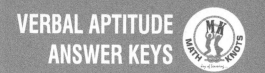

22.	A
23.	B
24.	A
25.	C
26.	B
27.	A
28.	C
29.	B
30.	D
31.	B
32.	A
33.	D
34.	C
35.	A
36.	D
37.	A
38.	D
39.	B
40.	B
41.	C
42.	D

www.math-knots.com

43. B

44. C

45. D

46. A

47. B

48. D

49. B

50. C

51. B

52. A

53. D

54. B

55. A

56. C

57. D

58. B

59. A

60. C

61. D

62. A

63. D

www.math-knots.com

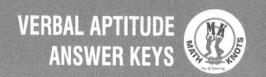

64.	B
65.	A
66.	C
67.	D
68.	A
69.	D
70.	B
71.	A
72.	C
73.	D
74.	B
75.	A
76.	C
77.	A
78.	A
79.	C
80.	B
81.	B
82.	D
83.	C
84.	D

85.	C
86.	B
87.	A
88.	D
89.	C
90.	A
91.	D
92.	B
93.	D
94.	A
95.	C
96.	B
97.	D
98.	A
99.	C
100.	A
101.	A
102.	D
103.	A
104.	B
105.	D

www.math-knots.com

106.	A	
107.	C	
108.	D	
109.	A ;	Types of things we wear or Garments
110.	A ;	All others are nature- bound, War is man-made
111.	C ;	All others are types of color
112.	D ;	All others are sense organs or related to sense organs
113.	B ;	Various types of gases
114.	D ;	Various expressions of joy
115.	A ;	Types of solid metals
116.	B ;	Various joints in human body
117.	D ;	Types of various professions
118.	C ;	Various types of instructors
119.	B ;	Various types of string instruments
120.	B ;	Various forms of running water
121.	D ;	Parts of tree above ground
122.	A ;	Various types of transportations
123.	C ;	Types of players in various sports
124.	D ;	Permission meanings
125.	B ;	Things made of wood
126.	A ;	Meanings of highest point

127. C ; Canoe is a boat ,others are resting places of birds are animals

128. D ; Various types of planets

129. A ; Various types of 2-D Pictures

130. B ; Various types of flying objects

131. D ; Various types of baby animals

132. A ; Various types of crawling animals

133. C ; Various types of vegetation

134. B ; Various types of indoor games

135. B ; Various types of payments

136. D ; Types of vegetables that grow under ground

137. A ; Various types of legal professionals

138 . C ; Only arrow needs a bow. Others are used by hand

139. B ; All months have 31 days

140. A ; Various types of milk Products

141. D ; Various meanings of foundation

142. C ; All are more than one in the human body

143. B ; Various types of outdoor games

144. A ; Various deserts across world

145. B ; Various continents

146. D ; Types of houses

www.math-knots.com

147.   A ;   All are more than one in the human body

148.   C ;   Branches of math

149.   C ;   Various currencies

150.   D ;   Same meaning

151.   B ;   Shades of Yellow

152.   A ;   Male animals

153.   D ;   Solid figures

154.   C ;   Types of looking; Wink is a momentary action

155.   D ;   Various types of positive feelings

156.   B ;   Things that girls wear on to their wrist / hand

157.   D ;   Various performers in movies, plays, skits etc..

158.   A ;   Milky way is a group of stars. All others are in sky as single entities

159.   B ;   Various types of fruits

160.   B ;   Various types of bugs not bug

161.   C ;   Various types of tenses

162.   D ;   Non-Metallic elements

163.   A ;   Various types of farming tools

164.   D ;   Shades of green. Crimson is a shade of red

165.   C ;   Same meaning

166.   B ;   House furnishings

       www.math-knots.com

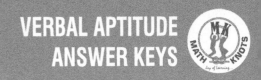

167.	D ;	Members of family blood relation
168.	A ;	Types of reptiles
169.	A ;	Various types of tools
170.	C ;	Names of various subjects
171.	D ;	Various tools to write
172.	B ;	Farming tools
173.	A ;	Various types of liquid measurements
174.	D ;	Various types of books to read
175.	A ;	Various insects
176.	C ;	Birds that can fly not swim
177.	C ;	Various types of distance measurements
178.	B ;	Last stage of any activity or process
179.	D ;	Various types of nuts
180.	A ;	Various types of branches of tree